LOST IN THE STARS

Maxwell Anderson

Lost in the Stars

The dramatization of Alan Paton's novel,

Cry, the Beloved Country

This is an Anderson House book

WILLIAM SLOANE ASSOCIATES, INC.

First Printing

PRINTED IN THE UNITED STATES OF AMERICA
THE MAPLE PRESS COMPANY, YORK, PA.

LOST IN THE STARS

Lost in the Stars

LEADER	HLABENI
ANSWERER	MARK ELAND
STEPHEN KUMALO	LINDA
GRACE KUMALO	MATTHEW KUMALO
NITA	JOHANNES PAFURI
STATIONMASTER	ABSALOM KUMALO
YOUNG MAN	ROSE
YOUNG WOMAN	IRINA
JAMES JARVIS	SERVANT
ARTHUR JARVIS	POLICEMAN
EDWARD JARVIS	WHITE MAN
JOHN KUMALO	WHITE WOMAN
PAULUS	THE GUARD
WILLIAM	BURTON
JARED	THE JUDGE
ALEX	PARISHIONERS
FOREMAN	MCRAE
MRS. MKIZE	VILLAGER
SINGERS	

Act One

SCENE I

e curtain goes up in darkness and a picture of the Ixopo hills develops adually in the background. From the orchestra pit a broad flight of steps ds up to the stage. A group of singers sits on these steps, so placed that they e not in the way of the action but can comment on it or ascend to take part it at any time. The first scene is the tiny and cheap but clean sitting room the home of Stephen Kumalo, near St. Mark's Church near Ndotsheni, tal, South Africa. As the curtain rises, we see SINGERS entering from the t onto the center stairs, and also from right and left stage to positions on the de steps. The LEADER takes his place center stage and sits on a basket which carries on stage.

1

LEADER   [*Sings*]
            There is a lovely road
            that runs from Ixopo into the hills.
            These hills
            are grass covered and rolling, and they are lovely
            beyond any singing of it.
            About you
            there is grass and bracken, and you may hear
            the forlorn crying of the titihoya bird.
            The grass of the veld is rich and matted.
            You cannot see the soil.
            The grass holds the rain and mist,
            and they seep into the ground, feeding
            the streams in every clove.
            The clove is cool and green and lovely beyond any singi
                of it.

ANSWERER But sing now about the lower hills.

LEADER   Where you stand the grass is rich and matted—
            but the rich green hills break down.
            They fall to the valley below—
            and, falling, change.
            For they grow red and bare;
            they cannot hold the rain and mist;
            the streams run dry in the clove.
            Too many cattle feed on the grass;
            it is not kept or guarded or cared for,
            It no longer keeps men, guards men, cares for men.
            The titihoya cries here no more.

ANSWERER Yes, wherever the hills have broken down and the red cl
            shows through, there poor people live and dig ever more de
            perately into the failing earth.

LEADER   [*Sings*]
            The great red hills stand desolate,
            and the earth has torn away like flesh.
            These are the valleys
            of old men and old women,
            of mothers and children.
            The men are away.

The young men and the girls are away.
The soil cannot keep them any more.

[STEPHEN KUMALO *enters and sits on a chair behind the table. As the last of the* SINGERS *go out the lights come up on the sitting room.* GRACE KUMALO, *Stephen's wife, enters, and a small Zulu girl,* NITA, *runs in with a letter and crosses to Stephen*]

NITA   [*Handing the letter to Stephen*] I bring a letter, umfundisi.

STEPHEN   Where did you get it, my child?

NITA   From the store, umfundisi. The white man asked me to bring it to you.

STEPHEN   That was good of you. Go well, small one.

[NITA *starts to go, but pauses*]

GRACE   Perhaps you might be hungry, Nita.

NITA   Not—not very hungry.

STEPHEN   Perhaps a little hungry?

NITA   Yes, a little hungry, umfundisi.

GRACE   There is a little bowl on the kitchen table, Nita. And a spoon beside it.

NITA   I thank you.

[NITA *goes to the kitchen; Stephen sits fingering his letter;* GRACE *crosses to him and looks over his shoulder at the letter*]

GRACE   From Johannesburg.

STEPHEN   Yes, August 9, 1949.

GRACE   "Reverend Stephen Kumalo, St. Mark's Church, Ndotsheni, Natal." It is not from our son.

STEPHEN   No. It's a writing I haven't seen.

GRACE   It may bring news of him.

STEPHEN   Yes. Let me think. Our son Absalom is in Johannesburg; m
sister Gertrude is there—and my brother John is there. B
he has never written to me.
[*He picks up the knife from the table*]
Perhaps the way to find out is to open it.
[*He slits the flap with the knife and hands the letter to Grace*]
Read it, my helper. Your eyes are better than mine.

GRACE   It's from your brother John.

STEPHEN   Then this is truly an occasion. Read carefully, my helpe

GRACE   "Dear Stephen, you old faker in Christ. I don't know wheth
it was you who sent our dear sister Gertrude to Johannesbu
or not, but if it was, for the love of your own Jesus send a
fetch her back. She says she came looking for a husband wh
ran away from her. Maybe so. Anyway she's found plen
husbands, and the stories about the kind of house she kee
are not good for my business, because it's known here who s
is. See to this soon, O brother in God, or I'll have the wom
put away where she won't be so noticeable. Your affectiona
brother, John." He's an evil man.

          [*She sits*]

STEPHEN   [*Humorously*] No, he honestly thinks that I am a faker. H
thinks all men are fakers, perhaps because he's one. But I a
not concerned about that. I am concerned about Gertrude
if she has taken to bad ways.

GRACE   What will you do?

STEPHEN   I don't know.

GRACE   [*She has a plan*] If you were in Johannesburg you could fi
Gertrude.

STEPHEN   It's many hundreds of miles. Where would I find the mon
to go to Johannesburg?

GRACE   There is the St. Chad's money.

PHEN   Absalom's money—the money we save for his school? You would have me use that?

ACE   Should you not, Stephen? Absalom will never go now to St. Chad's.

PHEN   How can you say that? How can you say such a thing?

ACE   He is in Johannesburg. When people go to Johannesburg they do not come back.

PHEN   But Absalom will! Absalom went to Johannesburg for one purpose—to earn money for his education! When he returns he will bring twelve pounds of his own to put with the twelve we have saved, and then he will have enough for a year at St. Chad's, and he will go there and learn quickly! I know him!

ACE   It's nearly a year since we had a letter from him, Stephen. We do not know him now. He has been in the mines. No young man could work in the mines and not change. Absalom will not go to school. Take the money—use it!

PHEN   Do you know what you are saying? If I take his school money and use it to bring Gertrude back, then I have given up Absalom! I have said by this action that he will not make a place for himself, that we shall not see him nor be proud of him again, that he is only a drop in the great river of blacks that pours into the earth and is seen no more! I will not say this! I will not think it!

ACE   I love him as much as you, but why has he not written to us? If there's nothing wrong he could have written.

PHEN   O mother of little faith! A letter can be lost so easily! We must not cease to believe in him. We must love him, and not doubt him. There's a great gulf between people, Grace, between husband and wife, between parents and child, between neighbor and neighbor. Even when you live in the same house it's deep and wide, except for the love between us. But when there is love, then distance doesn't matter at all—distance or silence or years.

[*He sings "Thousands of Miles"*]
How many miles
   To the heart of a child?
      Thousands of miles, thousands of miles.
When he lay on your breast
   He looked up and smiled
      Across tens of thousands,
      Thousands of miles.
Each lives alone
   In a world of dark,
Crossing the skies
   In a lonely arc,
Save when love leaps out like a leaping spark
   Over thousands, thousands of miles.

Not miles, or walls, or length of days,
   Nor the cold doubt of midnight can hold us apart,
For swifter than wings of the morning
   The pathways of the heart!
How many miles
   To the heart of a son?
      Thousands of miles, thousands of miles.
Farther off than the rails
   Or the roadways run
      Across tens of thousands,
      Thousands of miles
The wires and the ways,
   Reach far and thin
To the streets and days
   That close him in,
But there, as of old, he turns 'round to grin
   Over thousands—thousands of miles.

Not miles, or walls, or length of days,
   Nor the cold doubt of midnight can hold us apart,
For swifter than wings of the morning
   The pathways of the heart!
Over tens of thousands of miles.

[NITA *enters from upstage door*]

STEPHEN   Is the little bowl empty, Nita?

ᴀ   Yes, umfundisi. I thank you.

ᴘʜᴇɴ   Go well, my child.

ᴀ.   Stay well, umfundisi.

         [*She skips out and off left*]

ᴄᴇ   Stephen, please take the St. Chad's money. Go to Johannes-
         burg.

ᴘʜᴇɴ   You're not thinking of Gertrude. You're thinking of Absalom.

ᴄᴇ   Yes. We have heard nothing from our son for a year—go to
         Johannesburg. Find him.

ᴘʜᴇɴ   If you wish it so much, it may be that I should go, my helper.
         I shall bring you word of Absalom. It will be good news, that
         I know.
         [*He crosses left and looks at the clock*]
         I couldn't go today. The train goes at twelve, and it's past the
         hour. But I could go tomorrow.

ᴄᴇ   [*Her arms around him*] You are my Stephen.

         [*The lights dim*]

Act One

SCENE 2

The station at Carrisbrooke, indicated only by a semaphore. As the lights c
up a white STATIONMASTER *announces the coming of the train and a gr*
of ZULUS *enters, singing a farewell to one of their number who has*
called to work in the mines.

STATION- MASTER	Attention! The train for Johannesburg will be here in minutes! Have your baggage ready! Train for Johannesb
CHORUS	Johannesburg, Johannesburg. Johannesburg, Johannesburg.
LEADER	Train go now to Johannesburg, Farewell!
CHORUS	Farewell!
LEADER	Go well!
CHORUS	Go well!
LEADER	Train go now to Johannesburg, Farewell!
CHORUS	Farewell!
LEADER	Go well!
CHORUS	Go well! This boy we love, this brother, Go to Johannesburg! White man go to Johannesburg— He come back, he come back. Black man go to Johannesburg— Never come back, never come back!
YOUNG MAN	[*Speaking*] I come back.

8

OMAN   Please!

OUNG   All this they say—
AN   I fool them. I come back.

HORUS   [*Sings*]
            Black man go to Johannesburg—
            Go, go, never come back
            Go, go, never come back.
            Train go now to Johannesburg—
            Farewell, farewell,
            Go well, go well!
            This boy we love, this brother,
            Go to Johannesburg.
            White man go to Johannesburg,
            He come back, he come back.
            Black man go to Johannesburg,
            Go, go, never come back—
            Go, go, never come back, never come back
            Never come back!

            [JAMES JARVIS, *an Englishman of about fifty-five, enters, ac-
            companied by his son,* ARTHUR, *and his grandson,* EDWARD.
            They pause a minute to talk, the ZULUS *diminish their singing
            to a pianissimo*]

RTHUR   We're in plenty of time.

ARVIS   Yes—I can see the plume of smoke just over the hill. The
            train will be here in three minutes.

DWARD   I wonder who invented schools, and Latin grammar.

RTHUR   It's not only your school, son. I have to get back to work, too.

EDWARD   Anyway, I'll always remember this is the year I learned to
            ride horseback.

ARVIS   And I'll see that Danny gets his daily oats and exercise till
            you're here again. Next vacation you can wear longer stirrups
            and take a few jumps with him.

EDWARD   Do you think he'll remember me?

JARVIS   I'm not sure just how much a horse remembers. But he'll b
            here, and we'll all be here, waiting for you. The old place get
            pretty lonely with only your grandmother and me.

EDWARD   It was the best mid-term I ever had.

JARVIS   [*Smiling*] Thank you, Edward.
            [STEPHEN KUMALO *enters with his wife and crosses to center; h
            is carrying a small black bag*]
            It was among the best I ever had. You have a book to read o
            the train?

EDWARD   I have my Latin grammar—but I'm planning to look out th
            window a lot.

ARTHUR   There's Stephen Kumalo—and I haven't seen him for a year
            Forgive me.

            [*He starts toward Stephen*]

JARVIS   Arthur!

ARTHUR   Yes?

JARVIS   I don't know what the customs are now in Johannesburg
            They may have changed since I was there. But in our villag
            one does not go out of his way to speak to a black.

ARTHUR   The customs have not changed in Johannesburg, Father. Bu
            I am not bound by these customs. I have friends among the
            Zulus. And my friends are my friends.
            [*He goes to Stephen and offers his hand*]
            Mr. Kumalo!

STEPHEN   Ah, Mr. Jarvis!

            [*They shake hands*]

ARTHUR   You're making a journey?

STEPHEN   To Johannesburg, sir. It is my first long journey. And a
            happy one—I go to see my son!

ARTHUR   Ah! And Mrs. Kumalo goes with you?

RACE   No, sir. I stay with the house.

ARTHUR   I'm leaving today, too. I wish I'd had time to see you while
          we were here.

STEPHEN   Sir, it is always a great pleasure to see you. Perhaps when you
          come again—

ARTHUR   That's right—there's always a next time. And I won't forget.

          [ARTHUR *and* STEPHEN *shake hands again*]

STEPHEN   I know you won't, sir.

          [ARTHUR *returns to his father and son*]

JARVIS   If you had struck me across the face you couldn't have hurt
          me more—or damaged me more, in the eyes of those who
          stand here. I suppose you know that?

ARTHUR   I don't believe that, Father. This is an old quarrel between us.
          We haven't time to settle it before the train goes. Perhaps we
          shall never settle it.

JARVIS   What you do in Johannesburg I can't alter! But here, where
          every eye is on us, where you are known as my son, you could
          avoid affronting me in such a fashion! Will you remember
          that in the future?

ARTHUR   Let's shake hands and agree to disagree, Father. The train is
          almost here.

JARVIS   You make no promises?

ARTHUR   I make no promises.

JARVIS   Then I'm not sure that I want you to come here again, Arthur!

ARTHUR   Father!

JARVIS   I'm sorry. Of course you'll come again.

ARTHUR   Not if it offends you, Father. But—my friends are my friends

            [ARTHUR *and* JARVIS *face each other. The* CHORUS *begins*
            imitate the approaching train]

EDWARD   Good-by, Grandfather.

JARVIS   Good-by, Edward.

ARTHUR   Good-by, sir.

            [*He puts out his hand*]

JARVIS   Good-by, Arthur

            [*He shakes hands with Arthur.* ARTHUR *and* EDWARD *go to th*
            left. STEPHEN *has started to go toward the train off-stage lef*
            but steps back to let ARTHUR *and* EDWARD *precede him. A*
            STEPHEN *and his wife go out the* ZULUS *shout to them*]

LEADER   Go well, umfundisi.

STEPHEN   Stay well, you who dwell here.

            [*The* CHORUS *and the* LEADER, *imitating the train, sing simul*
            taneously]

LEADER   White man go to Johannesburg,
            He come back,
            He come back.

CHORUS   Clink, clink, clickety.

1ST VOICE   [*Imitating the whistle*] Whoo-oo-oo-oo!

CHORUS   Black man go to Johannesburg!
            Never come back, never come back!
            Clink, clink, clickety,
            clink, clink, clickety . . .

            [*The lights fade*]

Act One

John Kumalo's tobacco shop in Johannesburg. A counter with a small display of cigars, cigarettes, and tobacco. John is conferring with some political lieutenants, all Zulus or Bantu.

JOHN
Don't take it so hard, gentlemen, don't take it so hard. We won't get equal suffrage, we won't get social equality, we won't get any kind of equality—but those of us who are quick in the head will get along. That's the way it is everywhere, for whites and for Zulus. Use your head and you can live. Try to reform the world and somebody steals your mealies. Now—suppose a Zulu says to you, "I demand equality; I want to vote and I want to be represented!" What do you say to him? You, Paulus?

PAULUS
I say to him, "Man, our Political League is out for just that; it's out for equality. We won't get it this year. We won't get it next year. But we'll get it!"

JOHN
What else do you say to him? William?

WILLIAM
I say to him, "We've got a doctor in our League, brother. Somebody gets sick he goes to your house first. You run out of mealies maybe and need some to tide you over. Come and see me. We got a barrel in the back room just for that."

JOHN
That's right. Long-term notes, like equality, make 'em big—we're never going to pay. Short-term notes, like a bite to eat, keep 'em small. We pay 'em on the dot. And in ten years, gentlemen, our League will own Johannesburg.
[JARED, *a Zulu, enters*]
Yes, sir.

JARED
Some pipe tobacco, please.

JOHN
Native grown or imported?

JARED
Native grown. A quarter-pound.

[*He gets his tobacco and goes out*]
13

JOHN   And now, gentlemen, you're part of the biggest thing that's
            happening in this town!

            [STEPHEN KUMALO *enters, holding a small Zulu boy,* ALEX, *by
            the hand. John looks at Stephen without recognizing him*]

JOHN   Yes, umfundisi?

STEPHEN   I've come to see you, John . . .

JOHN   It's Stephen. It's our old gospel bird, scratching 'round in the
            big city. You got my letter?

STEPHEN   Yes. This is Gertrude's son. Little Alex.

JOHN   Excuse me, gentlemen. My own brother, the son of our
            mother, has come.
            [WILLIAM *and* PAULUS *go out*]
            Well, any rain down your way this year?

STEPHEN   Less than we needed, John.

JOHN   You should pray, brother, you should pray. Now about
            Gertrude, she goes back with you to Ndotsheni?

STEPHEN   She allows the child to go with me. But she stays here.

JOHN   Brother, I want our sister out of this town. There's a limit to
            the number of bastard nephews a respectable tradesman can
            have.

STEPHEN   I asked her to come with me. She would not. And she said,
            "John won't put me away anywhere. He would have to find
            me first, and he won't find me."

JOHN   You have failed with her.

STEPHEN   Yes.

JOHN   Take her son, then, and go back to your hills and your sheet-
            iron chapel and your rusty god. I thought you might rid me
            of the woman. If you can't do that I have no further use for
            you.

STEPHEN   Honest and straightforward, aren't you, John? I'll go, but first there are two things I must ask. I have no room to stay in—

JOHN   There's no room here.

STEPHEN   Don't be afraid. I can pay for a room.

JOHN   Perhaps I can find you one, then. What else?

STEPHEN   My son Absalom. Did you see him while he was here?

JOHN   How much have you heard from Absalom?

STEPHEN   Four letters—from the mines—nearly a year ago. He was well, and working hard.

JOHN   I see. Well—your son left the mines and went about with my son Matthew for a while. They both stayed here. But your Absalom was not a good influence on Matthew.

STEPHEN   John!

JOHN   I had to tell them to get out.

STEPHEN   You sent them away?

JOHN   Yes.

STEPHEN   Do you know—where they went?

JOHN   Yes, I've written it somewhere.

STEPHEN   I hoped you would know. That makes it all easy. Now I thank my God—I thank my *Tixo*—

JOHN   You can leave your God out of it. He's not interested. 14 Krause Street, Doornfontein Textiles Company.

STEPHEN   Doornfontein Textiles Company, 14 Krause Street.

JOHN   That's it. And now you want a place to stay.
[*He writes an address*]
You think I am a hard man.

STEPHEN   Brother, you have helped me. We do what we can.

JOHN   Brother, you're right. We do what we can. I hope you know
            what you do. You're the white man's dog, trained to bark
            and keep us in order. You know that.

STEPHEN   No, brother, I do not know it.

JOHN   They pile up mountains of gold, and they pay our sons three
            shillings a day, and out of this wage take a heavy tax. Is that
            fair?

STEPHEN   No, brother, it is not fair.

JOHN   Then why do you wear their Anglican clothes and read their
            Testament?

STEPHEN   Because all men do evil, I among them—and I wish all men
            to do better, I among them.

JOHN   [*Giving Stephen the address*] Yes, blessed are the chicken-
            hearted. This will give you a place to sleep. It's expensive and
            it's in Shanty Town and it's not pleasant. Such are the cus-
            toms of our city.

STEPHEN   I shan't mind. Good-by, John.

            [*He puts out his hand*]

JOHN   [*Taking it*] Good-by. You old faker in Christ.

STEPHEN   The same John!
            [*He starts out*]
            14 Krause Street. . . .

            [*The lights dim and go out*]

Act One

SCENE 4

he lights come up on the chorus on the orchestra pit steps.

CHORUS   [*Sings*]
14 Krause Street
    Textiles Company
14 Krause Street
    Textiles Company
14 Krause Street
    Textiles Company.

STEPHEN   [*Alone on the street*]
Not miles, or walls, or length of days,
    Nor the cold doubt of midnight can hold us apart,
For swifter than wings of the morning
    The pathways of the heart!

CHORUS   [*Sings*]
14 Krause Street
    Textiles Company
14 Krause Street
    Textiles Company.

[*Stephen is now seen speaking with a factory foreman who stands behind a cashier's cage. He is looking up a record in a large volume*]

FOREMAN   Yes, they did work here. Absalom Kumalo and Matthew Kumalo. But they left us some months ago.

STEPHEN   Sir, did they work well?

FOREMAN   Why, I think so. I rather liked Absalom. A good lad.

STEPHEN   Thank you, sir. He's my son, you know. Could you tell me where they went?

FOREMAN   They had a house address when they were here. They lived with Mrs. Mkize, 77 Twenty-third Avenue, Alexandra.

STEPHEN   Thank you, sir.

            [*The lights dim*]

CHORUS   [*Sings*]
            Seventy-seven, Twenty-third Avenue—
                Mrs. Mkize—Twenty-third Avenue.

            [*Stephen is now seen at a doorway.* MRS. MKIZE *appears in i*
            the lights come up.]

STEPHEN   How long ago, Mrs. Mkize?

MRS MKIZE   These many months.

STEPHEN   Do you know where he is now?

CHORUS   [*Sings*]
            Make no doubt
            It is fear that you see in her eyes!
            It is fear!

MRS MKIZE   No, I do not know.

STEPHEN   Are you afraid of me?

MRS MKIZE   No, I'm not afraid.

STEPHEN   But you tremble when I speak of him.

MRS MKIZE   I don't know you. I don't know why you ask.

STEPHEN   I am his father. I wish him well—and you well.

MRS MKIZE   His father? Then it would be better if you followed him
            further.

STEPHEN   Why?

MRS MKIZE   Umfundisi, they were friendly with a taxi driver nam
            Hlabeni who lives near the stand in this same street. At nu
            ber 25.

EPHEN   Why should I look no further?

RS MKIZE   Lest you be hurt by it.

EPHEN   What did he do?

RS MKIZE   In the middle of the night they brought things here, umfundisi. Clothes and watches and money. They left in haste.
I think they were near to being discovered. Oh, follow him no
further!

EPHEN   Hlabeni, at 25 on this street?

RS MKIZE   Yes.

[The lights dim]

ORUS   *[Sings]*
A taxi driver, known as Hlabeni,
     Taxi stand; in Twenty-third Avenue,
What you must find is always a number,
     A number and a name.
Though it sear the mind, say it over and over,
     Over and over,
     A boding song,
     Searing like flame.

ADER   *[Sings]*
Be there, my one son, be well there—

[Stephen is now at Hlabeni's doorway]

LABENI   I can tell you this much; they were picked up for something
they'd done, and one of them went to jail for a while.

EPHEN   What—had they done?

LABENI   Oh, some wild trick like boys do.

EPHEN   Which one went to prison?

LABENI   Absalom. I don't know why Matthew didn't go, but he got
out of it somehow. And Absalom's out now. He's on parole.
Or that's what I heard.

STEPHEN   Where would he be?

HLABENI   You could ask the parole officer at the government buildin
            He might know.

STEPHEN   Is it near?

HLABENI   Four or five miles.

STEPHEN   Could I find it tonight?

HLABENI   I'll tell you what I'll do. I'll draw you a map. That might hel

            [*The lights dim*]

CHORUS   [*Sings*]
            What you must find is always a number,
                A number and a name,
            In prison cells they give you a number,
                Tag your clothes with it,
                Print your shame!

LEADER   [*Sings*]
            Be there, my one son, be well there—

VOICE   [*Speaking*] But how could he be well there? How could he
            well?

            [*The lights come up on Stephen standing before Mark Elan*
            the parole officer, a young white man]

ELAND   Yes, he's been paroled, umfundisi. We made an exception i
            his case, partly because of his good behavior, partly becau
            of his age, but mainly because there was a girl who wa
            pregnant by him.

STEPHEN   He is married, then?

ELAND   No, umfundisi. But the girl seemed fond of him, so with a
            these things in mind—and with his solemn undertaking tha
            he would work hard to support the child and its mother—w
            let him go. He's living with the girl in Pimville.

EPHEN   Is it far?

AND   It's some miles. It's among the shacks there, and at night the streets are—well, pretty hard to get about in. I think I'd have to take you.

EPHEN   Could—could you go tonight, sir?

AND   Tonight I can't. But if you could come here early tomorrow—

EPHEN   Yes, sir. Thank you.

         [*The lights dim out*]

Act One

The lights come up as we see STEPHEN *striking a match and lighting candle in a tiny, squalid room. Alex is with him.*

ALEX   Uncle Stephen?

STEPHEN   Yes, Alex.

ALEX   The room is very small here, and not clean.

STEPHEN   Yes, it's the best they had.

ALEX   I hope we won't live here.

STEPHEN   No, no, Alex; you'll live in Ndotsheni. In the country. In m
            home.

ALEX   Is it like this there?

STEPHEN   No, not at all like this. There are hills and valleys, and tree
            growing on the hills and streams running in the valleys.

ALEX   What will our house be like?

STEPHEN   It's a little grey house.

ALEX   Will there be grass in front of it?

STEPHEN   Yes, and flowers growing in the grass.

ALEX   Do you have a wife there?

STEPHEN   Yes.

ALEX   I don't like my mother. She hits me. And I hit her, too
            Only she hits me harder!

STEPHEN   Nobody will hit you in my house.

x   Tell me about the house. Why is it grey?

PHEN   Because it has not been painted.

x   Is the water good when it comes from the tap, or do you have
         to boil it?

PHEN   There's no tap at all, boy. We get water from the spring.
         There's a tree that my son liked to climb. He built himself
         a place to sleep in it, like a nest. You will climb that tree.

x   Is the nest still there?

PHEN   Yes, it's there.

x   I see. I'm thinking about it.

         [*He looks out, imagining*]

RUS   [*Sings*]
         What are you thinking,
             Old man among the broken boxes
                 Of Shanty Town?

         What do you see,
             Child with the shining eyes,
                 Among the broken hopes
                     Of Shanty Town?

PHEN   [*Sings "The Little Grey House"*]
         There's a little grey house
             In a one-street town,
         And the door stands open,
             And the steps run down;
         And you prop up the window
             With a stick on the sill,
         And you carry spring water
             From the bottom of the hill;
         And the white star-of-Bethlehem
             Grows in the yard,
         And I can't really describe it
             But I'm trying hard;

It's not much to tell about,
It's not much to picture out,
   And the only thing special is
     It's home.

CHORUS   It's not much to sing about,
It's not much to picture out,
   And the only thing special is
     It's home.

STEPHEN It's a long road, God knows,
The long and turning iron road that leads to Ndotsheni.
How I came, God knows, by what ridges, streams, a
   valleys,
And how we shall return is in God's keeping.
Many bright days, many dark nights, we must ride on ir
Before I see that house again!

There's a lamp in the room,
   And it lights the face
Of the one who waits there
   In her quiet place,
With her hands always busy
   Over needle and thread,
Or the fire in the kitchen
   To bake tomorrow's bread.
And she always has love enough
   To take you in,
And her house will rest you
   Wherever you've been!

CHORUS   It's not much to tell about,
It's not much to picture out,
   And the only thing special is
     It's home!

STEPHEN It's not much to tell about,
It's not much to picture out,
   And the only thing special is
     It's home!

[STEPHEN *carries Alex up to the cot and covers him with a blan*
He blows out the candle. The lights dim out]

Act One

SCENE 6

A dive in Shanty Town. Some strange harmonies have crept into the last few bars and now we discover that they were indications of another song that begins to come from another part of the stage, still in darkness. It's sung in the manner of a night-club entertainer. The voice is a girl's. As the lights come up we see Linda, the singer, Matthew Kumalo, Johannes Pafuri, and Rose and Sutty, two girls who came with the young men. Absalom Kumalo sits alone and moody. Two DANCERS, *a man and a girl, dance to Linda's singing.*

LINDA   [*Sings "Who'll Buy"*]
Who'll buy
My juicy rutabagas?
Who'll buy
My yellow corn?
Who'll buy asparagus or carrots or potatoes?
Who wants my peppers and my ginger and tomatoes,
The best you bit into
Since you were born?
If you want to make a supper dish fit for a king
Look over what I offer, I offer everything!
So try my, buy my
Black-eyed peas;
The garden of Eden
Had nothing like these!
You'll feel like flying, like a bird on the wing;
You'll stay up there like a kite on a string:
They're satisfactory, and they got a sting!
So try my,
Buy my
Asparagus, yellow corn, black-eyed peas, tomatoes, potatoes,
    beans, and rutabagas—
Who'll buy
My oranges and melons?
Who'll buy
My prickly pears?
Who'll pay shillings for my lemons and persimmons,
Who wants apricots and nectarines and trimmin's,

The best you laid lip to
The last ten years?
I haven't got a license, so I can undersell,
I haven't got a license, so I treat you well!
So try my, buy my
Pure veld honey!
In the garden of Eden
They never use money!
You'll feel like flying, like a bat out of hell,
You'll own high heaven and a landing field as well!
The apples of Paradise, they always jell!
So try my—

MATTHEW,   Try my—
JOHANNES

LINDA   Buy my—

OTHERS   Buy my—

LINDA   Oranges, prickly pears, apricots, nectarines, tangerine
           apples, groundnuts, bananas—
           Buy my—

OTHERS   Buy my—

LINDA   Oh my—

OTHERS   Oh my—

LINDA   Oh my—

OTHERS   Oh my—

LINDA   Buy my—oh my—oh my—

JOHANNES   I'll take 'em! I'll take 'em all! You're off the market!

LINDA   [*Falling into Johannes' arms*] Sold!

MATTHEW   Just one little technical problem here if you don't mind, lady
           You said you had no license?

NDA   That's right. No license. Just Johannes' little wild honey, that's all.

ATTHEW Officer, arrest that woman and bring her before the court. [JOHANNES *brings* LINDA *down front as if to face the judge*] In the first place, what is a—h'm—rutabaga?

NDA   It's a vegetable, Your Lordship.

ATTHEW You don't give that impression.

NDA   What impression do I give, Your Lordship?

ATTHEW Are you trying to corrupt this court?

NDA   Yes, sir.

ATTHEW Twenty years, hard!

OHANNES Your Lordship, your wig is dirty, your logic is full of holes, and your monocle don't fit you!

ATTHEW I find you in contempt—hic! Damn that whisky and soda.

OHANNES What's the trouble, Your Monocle?

ATTHEW Young man, did you address me as Your Monocle?

OHANNES Yes, Your Monocle.

ATTHEW Forty years, hard!

OHANNES You got a little mixed here, Your Whisky and Soda! You're supposed to be trying this young lady!

ATTHEW That's right. [*To Rose, who is sitting on table*] Make a note the young man's right. Hic. Put in that hic. That was a British hic. Put it in.

OSE   [*Imaginary writing of notes*] Yes, sir!

ATTHEW Where's the persecution? Young man, will you persecute this young lady?

JOHANNES I'd love to, Your Rutabaga. When do I begin?

MATTHEW Woman, have you got anything to say?

LINDA I throw myself on the mercy of the court.

[*She throws herself into Johannes' arms*]

MATTHEW I'm the court, see! Throw yourself on me—not him!

ROSE I throw myself on the mercy of the court!

[ROSE *throws herself into Matthew's arms*]

JOHANNES I demand justice!

MATTHEW Remove that woman out of your pocket! And somebody scrape the court stenographer from the Judge's vest! Young man, you got justice, we all got justice! Justice is when the black man digs and the white man carries the brief case! Justice is when the black woman cooks and the white woman has breakfast in bed! If you want anything extra—you pay for it!

JOHANNES Your Honor, would you accept a little money?

MATTHEW What! Me, sir? A judge, sir? Take money, sir?—Yes, sir! All right, scrape her off your vest, Johannes! And get out of here, all of you! We'll be with you in a minute! Wait for us!

LINDA Where are we going to wait?

MATTHEW Outside!

LINDA Matthew!

MATTHEW Outside, I said!
[*They go, leaving Johannes, Absalom, and Matthew*]
Wake up, Absalom! Now to begin with—how do we get in?

JOHANNES You don't have to break into the house, I tell you; he never locks his doors, day or night.

MATTHEW   Why not?

JOHANNES   I don't know. He's got some theory. He says, "If anybody wants what I've got he can come in and take it."

ABSALOM   Then why would we need a gun when we go there?

MATTHEW   Because nobody ever knows when he's going to need a gun! And you've got a gun—and we might as well have it along!

ABSALOM   But Johannes says there won't be anybody there! The white man went for a trip somewhere and the servant gets home late every night.

MATTHEW   That's the way we think it's going to be, but if somebody happens to come in we don't want to take chances.

LINDA   [*Off stage*] Matthew!

MATTHEW   [*Calling*] We'll be right with you, pretty! [*To Absalom*] So don't come without it. We might need it. What do you say?

ABSALOM   I think it's better without the gun.

MATTHEW   Well, I don't, see? And if you don't bring it you're not in on this at all. Look, I'm going to get to those new gold fields! And I'm going on my own. Now, if you want to help us raise the money to get there, you're in; you come along! But if you're scared to carry that cheap revolver of yours you're no use to us. So bring it or stay home.

LINDA   [*Off stage*] Matthew!

MATTHEW   [*To Johannes*] We'll get rid of the girls. Think it over, country boy.

[JOHANNES *and* MATTHEW *go out to the right.* IRINA, *a young and pretty Zulu girl, enters from the left. She sees Absalom and crosses to him*]

IRINA   [*Timidly*] Absalom?

ABSALOM   Irina? What do you want?

IRINA   I came to tell you something.

ABSALOM   Yes?

IRINA   Something about the parole officer.

ABSALOM   What happened?

IRINA   He came to the cabin asking for you. And I lied. I had to lie.
             I told him you were at work and things were going well. But
             he'll be at the factory tomorrow—and if you're not there—

ABSALOM   I don't think I will be there.

IRINA   What will happen to you, Absalom?

ABSALOM   I won't be there. I won't be anywhere where he can find me.
             Ever again.

IRINA   What will happen to us? You and me?

ABSALOM   We'll live in a better place than Shanty Town.

IRINA   When?

ABSALOM   When I come back.

IRINA   Are you going away?

ABSALOM   Yes, but not from you! To get something for you and me!
             Look, Irina, suppose I went home with you now and went to
             work tomorrow. What kind of life would we have?

IRINA   Like others.

ABSALOM   Yes, like the others. Shanty Town. Crawling with boarders
             and bugs and children. You'd have your baby, and I'd keep
             on at the factory, and you'd have another baby, and we'd
             live in the same shack and pay our taxes and our rent and
             pretty soon we're sleeping four in a room. Ten in a room.
             Filth. Nothing. And that's our fun. That's our life forever.
             That's what we get. Isn't it?

IRINA   I'll keep our place clean, Absalom.

ABSALOM   Nobody can keep those places clean! And I can't stand it.
             I don't want it that way—I love you, Irina. I want you to
             have something better than that.

IRINA   What could we have?

ABSALOM   I've never been able to bring you a gift, Irina. We've always
             had—not quite enough to live on. Even the way we live. I
             want to come back with enough so we can set up a little shop,
             and be free of work gangs, and keep our own house—

IRINA   Where could you get money for this?

ABSALOM   In the new gold fields. There's a new rich strike, Irina. If
             you go there as a free man, not in a labor gang, you can some-
             times get ahead and save something—

IRINA   [Her arms about him] I'm afraid for you. Come home with me.

ABSALOM   Wait for me, Irina. I'll come home when I have something—
             when I am something.

IRINA   Where will you get money to go to the mines?

ABSALOM   We'll get it.

IRINA   You won't steal again?

ABSALOM   We'll get it.

IRINA   Oh, Absalom, Absalom, if you were caught once more they
             could keep you from me a whole lifetime! Come home with
             me, Absalom, come home with me!

ABSALOM   Oh, God damn this world!
             [He kisses her]
             Yes, I'll come with you.

             [They start out as MATTHEW, followed by JOHANNES, re-enters]

MATTHEW   Where you going, Absalom?
           [*He sees Irina*]
           It's his cook! It's his little cookie!

ABSALOM   I'm out of it.

MATTHEW   She gives the orders, huh? . . . You could be rich, you
           know—

ABSALOM   I'm on parole. You're not.

MATTHEW   One more black boy loose in a gold field, they'd never locate
           you.

ABSALOM   But even if we make money in the gold fields, we still have to
           come back here. And they'll get me.

MATTHEW   Why would they? You'll change your name, you'll be wearing
           new clothes, you'll have cash in your pocket, you can walk
           up and buy a shack of your own. There won't be any Absalom
           Kumalo. There'll be a new man! A man—not somebody's
           dumb ox!

ABSALOM   He's right, Irina—wait for me. It'll take a little time, but
           wait for me.

IRINA   Please—

ABSALOM   Go now, Irina. I'll be back.

IRINA   Oh, Absalom—

ABSALOM   Go, Irina!

IRINA   Yes, I'll go.

           [*She goes out*]

MATTHEW   That's more like it!

JOHANNES   You know what I heard? I heard there's sometimes loose gold
           you can pan out of a river if you get there before the land's
           all fenced.

TTHEW   Some places you can take just a kitchen pan and wash the dirt around in it and there's gold at the bottom.

IANNES   It's that way beyond Rigval clove.

TTHEW   And then, by God, we'll live like men! Johannes, you bring along that machinery you talked about?

IANNES   I've got it where I can pick it up quick.

TTHEW   Then pick it up, and pick up your feet! This is the best time.

     [*The lights dim as they go out*]

Act One

Irina's hut in Shanty Town. We see the interior of the hut and the ⟨...⟩ behind it. ELAND *enters, followed by* STEPHEN. ELAND *knocks at the do⟨...⟩*

ELAND   [*At the door*] Irina!

IRINA   [*Going to the door*] Come in, sir.

           [ELAND *and* STEPHEN *enter her room*]

ELAND   Thank you, Irina. This is the Reverend Stephen Kuma⟨...⟩ Irina, Absalom's father. I have told him about you, and ⟨...⟩ wishes to see you and to see Absalom. We'll go on from h⟨...⟩ to the factory. Absalom's there, of course?

IRINA   No, sir.

ELAND   But—when I was here—two days ago—

IRINA   Yes, sir. I lied to you.

ELAND   Where is he?

IRINA   I do not know. He's gone, I don't know where.

ELAND   This is another of my failures, then. They're like water. Th⟨...⟩ live together, they get a child, they engage to marry, a⟨...⟩ the next day both have forgotten.

STEPHEN   Could I be alone with her a moment?

ELAND   I'll wait.

           [*He goes out*]

STEPHEN   Irina?

IRINA   Yes—umfundisi.

34

EPHEN   Perhaps my son never spoke of me to you. We love him very much, his mother and I—and I have come to Johannesburg thinking I might find him. Would you help me to find him?

NA   Yes, umfundisi.

EPHEN   He has lived here with you for some time?

NA   Yes.

EPHEN   You were not married in the church?

NA   No, umfundisi.

EPHEN   And you are to have a child?

NA   Yes.

EPHEN   Why has he left you?

NA   I—do not know.

EPHEN   You distrust me?

NA   No, umfundisi.

EPHEN   Do you have a family?

NA   I have no one.

EPHEN   But you lived somewhere—before you met Absalom.

NA   I lived in Sophiatown.

EPHEN   Alone?

NA   [*Picking nervously at the back of a chair*] Nobody lives alone in Sophiatown.

EPHEN   You lived with your first—husband?

NA   Yes. With my first.

STEPHEN   How many have there been?

IRINA   Three.

STEPHEN   Three. And now you will seek a fourth.

IRINA   No. I wait for Absalom.

STEPHEN   I think you would do anything! You would go to anyone!
           am an old man, Absalom's father, but you would come to n
           if I asked you! Anything!

IRINA   No. I would not.

STEPHEN   You think an umfundisi is not a man? What if I desired you
           with my whole body? What if I desire you now?

IRINA   You?

STEPHEN   Yes. I.

IRINA   It would not be right.

STEPHEN   Was it right before?   With the others?

IRINA   No. It was not right.

STEPHEN   Then why would you not be willing with me?

IRINA   I do not know.

STEPHEN   Then you would be willing?
           [*She is silent*]
           Would you be willing?

IRINA   No, I do not know.

           [*She twists her hands, looks away*]

STEPHEN   [*Savagely*] Speak! Tell me!

IRINA   I could be willing.

PHEN Yes, you are a woman who would go to anyone.

NA Why did you come here? How would I know what you think
—or what you want? I don't know what power you have—
or what you will do! I'm alone here. I'm to have a child, and
Absalom is gone—
[*She sits on the chair in a passion of crying*]
and I love him! I want only Absalom. He brought me only
trouble—but I love him!

:PHEN [*After a pause*] Yes, I was wrong. I should not have put you
to such a test. Will you forgive me? We all do what we must
do. Not what we wish but what we can.
[*He crosses closer to her*]
Do you forgive me?

NA Yes, umfundisi.

:PHEN I will go now, Irina, but I will come again. I'm searching for
my son. If I find him I will come to tell you. My address is
on this paper.
[*He hands her a slip of paper*]
If he comes back to you, please let me know.

NA Yes, umfundisi.

[*He goes out*]

INA [*Sings "Trouble Man"*]
Since you came first to me,
 Dear one, glad one,
You bring all the worst to me,
 Near one, sad one;
There's trouble in your coming,
 Trouble in your laughter,
There's trouble in your going,
 And trouble after.

Since you were near to me,
 Lost one, mad one,
No other is dear to me,
 Loved one, bad one;

I love your dark silence,
    Love your bright laughter
I love the trouble you bring me,
    The crying after!

Trouble man, trouble man,
    Since you've been gone,
Somehow I manage
    Living here alone;
All day long
    You don't catch me weeping
But, oh, God help me
    When it comes time for sleeping,
    When it comes time for sleeping here alone!

Trouble man, trouble man, walking out there,
Maybe in a strange place, God knows where,
Maybe in a strange town, hurrying and walking,
Listen to my blood and my bones here talking,
Listen to the blood in my hands and feet,
Finding you out on a far, strange street;
Finding the footprints out where you ran,
Asking, "Aren't you coming home, trouble man?
Trouble man! Trouble man! Trouble man! Trouble man!"
Saying, "All day long you don't catch me weeping,
But, oh, God help me when it comes time for sleeping,
When it comes time for sleeping here alone!"
    Trouble man! Trouble man!

[*The lights dim*]

Act One

SCENE 8

...tchen in Arthur Jarvis' home. As the lights come up we see a SERVANT *...cing dishes on the pantry shelves. We then see* JOHANNES, ABSALOM, *...d* MATTHEW *entering from the left, handkerchiefs tied over their faces. ...hannes is carrying an iron bar, Absalom carries a revolver.*

...VANT   [*Turning as he hears the noise of their entrance*] What do you want?

...ANNES   We want money and clothes!

...VANT   It's Johannes! I know you! You cannot do such a thing!

...ANNES   Do you want to die?

...VANT   [*Running to the door and opening it*] Master! Master!

> JOHANNES *strikes the servant over the head with the iron bar; the* SERVANT *falls.* ARTHUR JARVIS *comes into the doorway,* ABSALOM *fires the revolver.* ARTHUR JARVIS *falls to the floor*]

...TTHEW   Quick! Get out!

> [*The three run to the left, stop in panic, turn and run off to the right. The lights go out*]

...ORUS   [*Sings "Murder in Parkwold"*] Murder in Parkwold!

...MAN   [*Speaking*] He was shot at night!

...ORUS   Murder in Parkwold!

...MAN   [*Speaking*] Nobody knows why or by whom!

...ITES   Murder in Parkwold!

...N   [*Speaking*] There was one shot only!

39

CHORUS   Murder in Parkwold!

WOMAN   [*Speaking*] He went to help the servant!

CHORUS   Murder in Parkwold!

MAN   [*Speaking*] The servant had called out!

WHITES   Murder in Parkwold!

CHORUS   Murder in Parkwold!

ALL   In Parkwold, among the great houses,
            Among the lighted streets and the wide gardens.

WOMAN   [*Speaking*] There are not enough police!

            [*The lights dim. The* CHORUS *goes out. From off-stage right con
            a man's voice singing*]

MAN   Murder in Parkwold!

ANOTHER   [*Off-stage left*] Murder in Parkwold!

            [*The lights come up immediately on the next scene*]

Act One

SCENE 9

Arthur Jarvis' library. As the lights come up we see James Jarvis seated in a chair by a desk, motionless and alone. ELAND *knocks and then enters.*

ELAND   Mr. Jarvis? Mr. Jarvis?

JARVIS   [*Looking up*] Yes, Eland.

ELAND   I could come later if I disturb you.

JARVIS   No—no.   Come in.

ELAND   I have seen the police. They have arrested Pafuri, the one who used to work in your son's house—and he has been identified.

JARVIS   By whom?

ELAND   By the servant who was struck.

JARVIS   I think I remember the name. Pafuri. Johannes Pafuri. Yes, he was houseboy here. I suppose he could be guilty—not that it would help to fix the guilt. Our son is dead. Arthur is dead and punishment will not bring him back.

ELAND   This boy denies being involved, but he looks very guilty.

JARVIS   One thing I hope the police will remember; no man is to be punished unless guilty.

ELAND   They'll make very certain before they act, Mr. Jarvis. They assured me of that.

JARVIS   I differed sharply with my son concerning our policy toward the blacks, but in this I want what he would have wanted—that the guilty feel the penalty—no man else. I had quarreled with my son, I suppose you know that. I wish we'd had a chance to patch up that quarrel.

ELAND   I'm sure it wasn't serious.

41

JARVIS   Yes. It was serious. Over Negro equality.
            [*He rises*]
            And the irony of it, that an advocate of Negro equality
            should have been killed by a Negro. There's only one course
            with them—a strong hand and a firm policy. They under-
            stand nothing but discipline, respect nothing else.

ELAND   There are good and bad among them.

JARVIS   Are there? At this moment I wonder.

ELAND   We can know them only by their actions. There was a man
            who came into this house with a pistol, came with intent to
            steal, and ended by committing murder. Let us find this one
            man and see that he is punished. Let us not blame the whole
            race.

JARVIS   You think he will be found?

ELAND   He will be found.

JARVIS   May he suffer as we suffer. As my wife suffers now.

ELAND   There's something I wanted to ask you, Mr. Jarvis. If you'd
            rather not stay in this house—

JARVIS   I want to stay here. This is where he worked. He was here
            when he heard the cry from the kitchen and ran to help.

ELAND   He will be a great loss to us. To our country and to me per-
            sonally. As a parole officer—well, many times I'd have given
            up in despair except for him.

JARVIS   And yet they killed him. What would he have said about a
            crime like this?

ELAND   He would have said, "They live in such poverty and fear.
            They see no way out of their poverty or their fear and they
            grow desperate."

JARVIS   Yes.
            [*He sits*]
            It sounds like him.

LAND   You wish to be here alone?

RVIS   Yes—I wish to be here alone.

          [*The lights dim.* ELAND *goes out. Off stage we hear again the cries repeated*]

AN   [*Sings, off-stage right*] Murder in Parkwold!

NOTHER   [*Sings, off-stage left*] Murder in Parkwold!

Act One

A street in Shanty Town. As the lights come up the street is empty. A MAN
and a WOMAN *run through, knocking at doors. The* ZULUS *come out of their
houses and gather in groups around three newspapers, reading intently.
There is a whistle from off right—the street empties, and the houses go dark.
A* POLICEMAN *passes through, disappears. The people emerge from the
houses, cluster again around the papers. A* WHITE MAN *and* WOMAN
enter from the right.

WOMAN   These streets are full of evil; I'm afraid!

MAN   It's all right, take my arm. This is a shabby neighborhood.

WOMAN   Hush!
       [*The* POLICEMAN *re-enters from left and meets the couple center
       stage. The* WOMAN *speaks with relief*]
       Good evening, officer.

       [*The* POLICEMAN *and the* WHITE COUPLE *go out left. The
       * NEGRO CHORUS *sings*]

1ST MAN   It is fear!

2ND MAN   It is fear!

1ST
WOMAN   It is fear!

3RD MAN   It is fear!

2ND MAN   Who can enjoy the lovely land,
       The seventy years,
       The sun that pours down on the earth,
       When there is fear in the heart?

       [*A group of* WHITE SINGERS *enters*]

WHITE
MAN   Who can walk quietly in the dusk
       When behind the dusk there are whispers
       And reckless hands?

WHITE   Yes, we fear them.
CHORUS   For they are many and we are few!

NEGRO   Who can be content
QUARTET   When he dares not raise his voice?

WHITE   It is fear!
CHORUS

NEGRO   For fear of the whip, the guard, the loss of his house?
QUARTET

WHITE   It is fear!
CHORUS

NEGRO   For fear of the mines,
CHORUS   And the prison,
            And the cell from which there is no return?
            Yes, we fear them,
            Though we are many and they are few!

WHITE   Who can lie peacefully abed
            When the dark without window is troubled
            By those who hate you for what you are and what you do?

NEGRO   You think you know what it is to fear or to hate?
            What is there you have not taken from us except hate and
                fear?
            Yes, we fear them, though we are many and they are few!

WHITE   Men are not safe in the streets,
            Not safe in their houses.

NEGRO   It is fear!

WHITE   There are brutal murders.

NEGRO   It is fear!

WHITE   Robberies!

NEGRO   It is fear!

WHITE   Tonight again a man lies dead!

NEGRO   Yes, it is fear!

WHITE   Yes, it is fear!

NEGRO   Fear of the few for the many!

WHITE   Fear of the few for the many!

NEGRO   It is fear!

WHITE   It is fear!

NEGRO   It is fear!

WHITE   It is fear!

ALL   Fear of the few for the many,
           Fear of the many for the few!

           [*The lights go out*]

Act One

SCENE II

The lights come up on ELAND, *who is pacing up and down.* STEPHEN *enters from the right, crosses to Eland.*

STEPHEN   I came as soon as I could, sir. You say—my son is here? Absalom is here?

ELAND   Yes.

STEPHEN   Why is he here?

ELAND   It's not proved, of course—but the charge is that he killed Arthur Jarvis.

STEPHEN   He killed—

ELAND   It could not be worse. For me or you or him. Forgive me. What I feel is nothing—I know that. Only it's my life work to help. And this may destroy it all.

STEPHEN   Absalom is accused of killing Arthur Jarvis?

ELAND   Remember, it's not proved about Absalom, and I don't believe it! It cannot be true.

STEPHEN   Let me speak to Absalom.
[*The lights come up on center stage; we see Absalom sitting on a stool in a cell, facing away from the entrance*]
My child, my child!

ABSALOM   [*Turning*] My father!

STEPHEN   At last I have found you.

ABSALOM   Yes, my father.

STEPHEN   I have searched in every place for you—and I find you here. Why have they charged you with this terrible crime? [*There is no answer*] Answer me, my child.

[*Absalom is still silent*]

ELAND   You should rise when your father speaks to you, Absalom.

ABSALOM   Yes, sir. Oh, my father, my father!

[*He reaches tnrough the bars to his father*]

STEPHEN   My son, my son, if I had only come sooner! But we shall make it all well yet, Absalom; for the courts are just, and when they have found that you did not kill it will be only a light punishment. [ABSALOM *drops his father's hands*] And when it ends you will come back to Ndotsheni and be content in our quietness. For you were a boy without guile and without anger, at home where there are hills and trees, not in these streets where men must live by their wits and without scruple. The hills are as beautiful as ever, Absalom. You will be happy there again.

ABSALOM   My father—

STEPHEN   Yes? [*Silence*] Yes?

ABSALOM   I cannot say it.

STEPHEN   I know you so well, Absalom, that I know you could not be guilty of this crime, and so you need not fear what the judge will say. You will live again at Ndotsheni.

ABSALOM   I shall never come home.

STEPHEN   Why, my son?

ABSALOM   Because I am guilty.

STEPHEN   Of what, my son?

SALOM   [*After a pause*] I killed the white man.

PHEN   But—this **cannot be true.** He was shot—in his house.

SALOM   Yes.

AND   There are three men accused in this murder, Absalom. Do you try to shield someone?

SALOM   No, sir. There were three of us, Matthew Kumalo and Johannes Pafuri and I. It was Johannes who struck the servant, but it was I who carried the revolver, and—

PHEN   And—you killed this man?

SALOM   I did not mean to kill him. We thought he would not be there. Then suddenly he was there, and I was frightened—and—

    [*A* GUARD *comes into the shadow from the right*]

AND   It is time for us to go.

PHEN   My son, I stand here, and see you, and a kind of dizziness has come over me, so that I am not sure what is real, or whether this is a true place or in a dream. Did you tell me, you, my son Absalom, that you had—had killed—a man?

SALOM   Yes, my father, it is true.

ARD   I'm sorry, umfundisi, it's time for you to go.

PHEN   May I come again?

ARD   Yes, umfundisi. At certain hours on certain days. The hours are ended for this day.

PHEN   Absalom—

SALOM   Yes, my father.

PHEN   Stay well, my child.

SALOM   Go well, my father.

    [STEPHEN *turns to go. The lights fade*]

Act One

The lights come up on Stephen in his Shanty Town lodging, where he .
at a table trying to write. ALEX, *in the cot near him, wakes and speaks*

ALEX   Uncle Stephen?

STEPHEN   Yes, Alex.

ALEX   Is it very late?

STEPHEN   Yes, very late.

ALEX   But you are not asleep.

STEPHEN   No. I must write a letter.

ALEX   Do you know the best thing that ever happened to me?

STEPHEN   No.

ALEX   These shoes you bought me, with the brass toes and t
          brass heels. Would it be all right if I kept them in bed wi
          me?

STEPHEN   If they're clean.

ALEX   I cleaned them on the quilt. I can see my face in the bra
          I could walk all the way to Ndotsheni wearing these sho

STEPHEN   Please, Alex, lie and sleep. Or be silent. This is a hard lett

ALEX   Who do you write to, Uncle Stephen?

STEPHEN   I write to my wife in Ndotsheni. To the mother at home.
          Tixo, Tixo! O God of all lost people and of those who
          toward death, tell me what to say to her! How can I say t
          to the mother, O my *Tixo?* That he has done this thing! Th
          I cannot bring him home! That he will perhaps never, nev
          come home!

50

ex   Uncle Stephen—who will not come home?

PHEN   My son Absalom.

ex   But Uncle Stephen, you are an umfundisi, and you can ask
          God to help you, and he will surely help you.

PHEN   I don't know, Alex.
          [*He sings "Lost in the Stars"*]
          Before Lord God made the sea and the land
          He held all the stars in the palm of his hand,
          And they ran through his fingers like grains of sand,
              And one little star fell alone.

          Then the Lord God hunted through the wide night air
          For the little dark star on the wind down there—
          And he stated and promised he'd take special care
              So it wouldn't get lost again.

          Now a man don't mind if the stars grow dim
          And the clouds blow over and darken him,
          So long as the Lord God's watching over them,
              Keeping track how it all goes on.

          But I've been walking through the night and the day
          Till my eyes get weary and my head turns grey,
          And sometimes it seems maybe God's gone away,
          Forgetting the promise that we heard him say—
          And we're lost out here in the stars—
          Little stars, big stars,
          Blowing through the night,
          And we're lost out here in the stars.

EPHEN,   Little stars,
ORUS   Big stars,
          Blowing through the night,
          And we're lost out here in the stars.

                        CURTAIN

Act Two

e curtain goes up on a dark and bare stage. The CHORUS *enters in the* *rk. The lights come up after the music has begun.*

ADER,
ORUS

[*Singing "The Wild Justice"*]
Have you fished for a fixed star
　　With the lines of its light?
Have you dipped the moon from the sea
　　With the cup of night?
Have you caught the rain's bow in a pool
　　And shut it in?
Go hunt the wild justice down
　　To walk with men.

Have you plotted the high cold course of a heron's flying,
Or the thought of an old man dying,
Or the covered labyrinth of
Why you love where you love?
Or, if one love you,
Why your love is true?
Only for a little, then,
Tease the wild justice down to dwell with men.

When the first judge sat in his place
And the murderer held his breath
With fear of death in his face,
Fear of death for death,
And all that could be said, for and against, was said,
And the books were balanced, and two, not one, were dead,
Was justice caught in this net?
Not yet, no, not quite yet, not yet.

No, tug first at the fixed star
　　On the lines of its light,
Sieve the moon up out of the sea
　　With the black seine of night,
Snare first the rain's bow in a pool
　　And close it in.

The wild justice is not found
   In the haunts of men.
The wild justice is not found in the haunts of men!

*[The lights come up on John's tobacco shop. John stands behi[
the counter, Stephen sits before him]*

JOHN   When you go before a judge you have to have a lawyer. N[
a lawyer's paid to lie and make it sound like the truth. I
getting a good lawyer. A white man's lawyer. And he'll do
he can for all three. There's no use trying to defend one alo[
—they all have to stick together in this. If they do that ther[
a good chance, because the fact is there's not much eviden[
against them.

STEPHEN   There's an identification, by the servant.

JOHN   Well, when our lawyer gets through with that, maybe n[
You see, the only one the servant says he identified is Johann[
Pafuri. He says he knew him because of his eyes. He's go[
peculiar twitch over his eye, and the servant could see [
eyes, even with the mask on—so he says he's sure it w[
Johannes. On the other hand, suppose it was somebody e[
with a twitch over his eye? With the rest of his face covered[
would be hard to be sure it was Johannes, wouldn't it? We
the lawyer will bring that up. And that'll shake the identific[
tion. And there's no other evidence against them, positive[
none.

STEPHEN   Except that—they were there. They will have to say th[
they were there.

JOHN   Why?

STEPHEN   Because it is the truth.

JOHN   The truth! Why would they tell the truth in a court? Do th[
want to get themselves hanged? No, if they all say they kn[
nothing about it, they'll get off, as sure as God's got whiske[

STEPHEN   But in a court there is a plea—guilty or not guilty.

JOHN   Yes. They'll plead not guilty. Everybody does.

PHEN   But Absalom says he will plead guilty.

N   Good God! Why?

PHEN   Because he is guilty.

N   Look, Stephen, if they don't all tell the same story, anything can happen to them. Surely you see that. Let them prove the boys guilty if they can. It's not up to the defense to hand 'em their case on a platter.

PHEN   I haven't told Absalom what to say. But he says he will not lie again. That he's done his last evil, and from now on he won't tell a lie or do any wrong. And so he will tell them that he was there. And that he shot Arthur Jarvis.

N   Will he tell them Matthew was there—and Johannes?

PHEN   Yes.

N   Well—that changes everything. You better fix that, brother, and fix it fast, or I give you my word we'll fix Absalom. Talk to him, brother.

PHEN   I have. He will plead guilty.

N   A man who pleads guilty to murder receives the punishment of the first degree—and that's hanging by your neck with a sack over your head. They don't fool about that.

PHEN   He has already made a confession. He has admitted the whole charge.

N   He can deny that. He can say he was out of his mind—anything.

PHEN   And Matthew and Johannes will plead not guilty?

N   Of course they will. That's part of the game. This is what happens in a court, Stephen. The defendant may be guilty as hell but he goes in and pleads not guilty and his lawyer tries to make the evidence look as if he's not guilty. The prosecution may be weak as hell but it goes in and tries to make things look as if the defendant's guilty as a hyena. Each one tries

to foul up the witnesses on the other side and make his o
witnesses look good. If the defense piles up the most poi
why fine, the old sheep-face of a judge says he's not guilty
the prosecution piles up the most points, why old sheep-f
says hang him up. It's a game. Truth has nothing to do w
it. Now if Absalom pleads guilty it would make it look
for all three—but don't let him do it, brother, because
going to get Matthew out of this, and anything Absalom s
is going to be used against him. By me, if necessary. So t
to him, Stephen, talk to him as you never talked to anybc
before. He doesn't want to die—and you don't want him
die. If you want him to live, tell him to plead not gui

[*The lights dim.* JOHN *goes out. Stephen is left musing al*

STEPHEN   [*Sings "The Soliloquy"*]
           What have I come to here,
           At this crossing of paths?
           Must he tell a lie and live—
           Or speak truth and die?
           And, if this is so,
           What can I say to my son?
           O *Tixo, Tixo*, help me!

           Often when he was young
             I have come to him and said,
           "Speak truly, evade nothing, what you have done
             Let it be on your head."

           And he heeded me not at all,
             Like rain he ran through my hands,
           Concealing, as a boy will, taking what was not his,
             Evading commands.

           For he seemed to hear none of my words;
             Turning, shifting, he ran
           Through a tangle of nights and days,
           Till he was lost to my sight, and ran far into evil—
           And evil ways,
           And he was stricken—
           And struck back,
           And he loved, and he was desperate with love and fear a
               anger,

And at last he came
To this—
O God of the humble and the broken—
O God of those who have nothing, nothing, nothing—
To this—
To the death of a man!
To the death of a man!

A man he had given to death.
    Then my words came back to him,
And he said, "I shall do no more evil, tell no more untruth;
    I shall keep my father's ways, and remember them."

And can I go to him now
    And say, "My son, take care,
Tell no truth in this court, lest it go ill with you here;
    Keep to the rules, beware"?

And yet if I say again,
    "It shall not profit a man
If he gain the whole world and lose his own soul,"
    I shall lose Absalom then.
    I shall lose Absalom then.
[*He speaks*]
I must find some other way—
Some other hope.
My son did not mean to kill his son,
Did not mean to kill.
[*He sings*]
O *Tixo*, *Tixo*, help me!
[*He speaks*]
To whom can I appeal?
[*He sings*]
O *Tixo*, *Tixo*, help me!
[*He speaks*]
Where can I turn now?
[*He sings*]
O *Tixo*, *Tixo*, help me!

[*The lights dim out, and come up on the door of a well-kept resi-
dence in Johannesburg.* STEPHEN *goes to the door, knocks, gets
no answer, and starts to go.* JAMES JARVIS *opens the door*]

JARVIS   Yes? Did you knock?

STEPHEN   I—I'm sorry, sir. I—expected a servant to answer—I—

JARVIS   There are no servants here today, umfundisi. Did you wish
            see one of them?

STEPHEN   No, umfundisi. I wished to see you.

JARVIS   Yes?

STEPHEN   I—
            [*His body fails him. His cane clatters to the ground and he
            on the step.* JARVIS *comes down to him*]
            Forgive me, umnumzana—

            [*His hat lies beside him, he reaches for it, leaves it*]

JARVIS   Are you ill, umfundisi?

            [STEPHEN *doesn't answer, he is trembling, looking at the grou*
            finally he looks up and speaks]

STEPHEN   Forgive me—I—shall recover.

JARVIS   Do you wish water? Or food, perhaps? Are you hungry?

            [STEPHEN *reaches for his cane, with another effort gets to his f*
            JARVIS *stands watching him, finally picks up his battered old*
            and hands it to him]

STEPHEN   Thank you, sir. I am sorry. I shall go now.

JARVIS   But you said you wished to see me.

STEPHEN   Yes, sir.

JARVIS   Well, then—?

STEPHEN   I have no words to say it.

JARVIS   You are in fear of me. I do not know why.

EPHEN   I cannot tell it, umnumzana.

RVIS   I wish to help whenever I can. Is it so heavy a thing?

EPHEN   It is the heaviest thing of all my years.

RVIS   You need not be afraid. I try to be just.

EPHEN   Umnumzana—this thing that is the heaviest thing of all my years—it is also the heaviest thing of all your years.

RVIS   You can mean only one thing. But I still do not understand.

EPHEN   [*Slowly*] It was my son that killed your son.

         [JARVIS *turns and walks away—then comes back to Stephen*]

RVIS   Why did you come?

EPHEN   There were three who went to rob the house, umnumzana. Two of them have lied and said they were not there. My son has told truth, that he was there, that he fired the revolver that killed your son. He will die for this truthtelling, the lawyer thinks.

RVIS   Not for his truthtelling.

EPHEN   Umnumzana, could you intercede for him?

RVIS   One does not seek to influence a court.

EPHEN   He did not mean to kill. And he tells truth. Is there not a core of good in him who tells truth?

RVIS   My son left his doors always open. He trusted his fellow men. And for this your son killed him.

EPHEN   He never meant to kill. But the revolver was in his hand and he heard someone coming and was frightened.

RVIS   Have you thought what it is for me that my son is dead?

EPHEN   I have tried. I have thought of—my son—

JARVIS   Have you thought what it is for his mother? His mother v
            die of this. It's in her face.

STEPHEN   I know. I can see the face of my son's mother. Forgive r
            umnumzana—I know what this is to you. But—if he w
            only to live—even shut up—even far from us.

JARVIS   I try to be just. I know what it is to lose a son. But—I s
            again—one does not try to influence a court. And even if
            judge were merciful, mercy can be pitiless. If your son we
            free ten thousand others might be misled into the death
            escaped. Better that one be punished where punishment
            deserved—and the ten thousand be warned.

STEPHEN   I think he did not mean evil, umnumzana. And to die—wl
            he is loved—

JARVIS   I know about death.

STEPHEN   If I could take him back to his home, umnumzana! Aw
            from Johannesburg. He grew up in Ndotsheni. Among
            hills. There was no evil in him then. From our house we co
            see up through the clove to your great house. You were ki
            to the folk who worked the little farms. Be kind again. A t
            rible thing has befallen my people. We are lost. Not ma
            have found their way to the Christ, and those who have i
            are lost. My son was lost. This would not have happened
            there were not the gold mines, and the great city your peo
            have built, and the little hope we have.

JARVIS   Umfundisi, there are two races in South Africa. One is capa
            of mastery and self-control—the other is not. One is born
            govern, the other to be governed. One is capable of cult
            and the arts of civilization—the other is not. The differer
            between us is greater than that I live on a hill and you live
            the valley. If my son had killed your son I would not ha
            come to you for mercy. Nor to the judge. Whether it were
            son or yours, I would have said, let him answer the law!

STEPHEN   You—you could save him—

JARVIS   You have neither heard nor understood me! There is only
            handful of whites in South Africa to control the great tide

blacks—and the blacks have no control of their own! They have no mind to it—and no mind for it! It's their way to run and evade and lie and strike down in the dark! Those who will not keep order must be kept in order! Those who lift their hands to kill must know that the penalty for death is death!

STEPHEN   [*Humbly*] Umnumzana—I read my Testament carefully. Jesus has not said this.

JARVIS   No, he has not, but where there is government it's true. Have you more to say to me?

STEPHEN   No, umnumzana.

[JARVIS *turns to go in. The lights dim*]

Act Two

The lights come up on Irina's hut. We see IRINA *hanging some clothes on clothesline.*

IRINA   [*Sings "Stay Well"*]
       If I tell truth to you,
         My love, my own,
       Grief is your gift to me,
         Grief alone,
       Wild passion at midnight,
         Wild anger at dawn,
       Yet when you're absent
         I weep you gone.

       Stay well, O keeper of my love,
       Go well, throughout all your days,
       Your star be my luckiest star above
       Your ways the luckiest ways.
       Since unto you my one love is given,
       And since with you it will remain,
       Though you bring fear of hell, despair of heaven,
       Stay well, come well to my door again.

       [STEPHEN *enters from the left, knocks and then calls*]

STEPHEN   Irina?

IRINA   Yes?

STEPHEN   The trial will begin tomorrow. Do you wish to be there?

IRINA   Could I see him?

STEPHEN   Yes. All those in the court will see him.

IRINA   Then I wish to go. Umfundisi—is anything sure?

STEPHEN   Nothing is sure. He will be tried. It's not known what wil
come of it.

.INA   He might go free?

TEPHEN   I wish I could say yes. He says he will plead guilty. He says he will speak the truth. If he does I think he will stay in the prison. For a long time.

RINA   For a long time.

TEPHEN   For a very long time.

RINA   So that I will never see him?

TEPHEN   It may be many years.

RINA   Many years.

TEPHEN   Would you wait for him—if it were so long?

RINA   Yes, umfundisi. I would wait.

TEPHEN   He has asked me—would you wish to marry him in the prison—so that your child will have his name?

RINA   Yes.

TEPHEN   He wishes it.

RINA   [*Running to him*] Umfundisi—

TEPHEN   Yes?

RINA   Will they kill him?

TEPHEN   It's not known yet.

RINA   I want him to live! I want him to come back to me!

TEPHEN   Even if it's many years?

RINA   Yes.

STEPHEN   And you will wait?

IRINA   Yes.

STEPHEN   Even if he does not come back at all?

IRINA   I will still wait.

STEPHEN   And when the desire is on you?

IRINA   I desire only him.

STEPHEN   [*Stroking her hair*] I will come tomorrow for you. And I wi
             tell him that you wish the marriage. Stay well, Irina.

IRINA   Go well, my father.
             [STEPHEN *goes out.* IRINA *sings* "*Stay Well*"]
             When you have fled from me,
                 My love, my own,
             I've waited quietly,
                 Here alone.
             Some come back at midnight,
                 Or come back at dawn,
             Now that you're absent
                 I weep you gone.

             Go well, though wild the road and far
             Stay well through darkening days,
             Your star be still my luckiest star,
             Your ways the luckiest ways,
             Though into storm your lone bark be driven,
             Though my eyes ache for you in vain,
             Though you bring fear at dawn, despair at even,
             Stay well, come well to my door again.

             [*The lights dim*]

Act Two

courtroom. The judge's bench is at the left; the judge is seated. Absalom
d Matthew are in the prisoner's dock. In the courtroom are all those
e have seen who are concerned with this case or related to the prisoners:
ina, Linda, John, Stephen, the servant, and many Zulu spectators. James
rvis, Eland, and a number of whites sit on the opposite side of the court-
om. As the lights come up Johannes Pafuri is in the witness box, center,
d Burton, the defense lawyer, is questioning him.

JRTON   Johannes, you have been identified as one of three masked
men who entered the kitchen of Arthur Jarvis on October
eighth, between eleven and twelve. Were you there at that
time?

JHANNES   No, sir.

JRTON   Where were you?

JHANNES   At Mrs. Ndela's house, in End Street.

JRTON   How do you know you were there at eleven?

JHANNES   Because we had been dancing at a place in High Street till
nearly eleven, and at eleven we were at Mrs. Ndela's.

JRTON   Who else was there?

JHANNES   Matthew Kumalo was there, and the girls Linda and Rose.

JRTON   The witness is excused. Will Matthew Kumalo take the stand?
[MATTHEW KUMALO *comes down into witness box*]
Matthew Kumalo, you are accused of being one of three
masked men who entered the kitchen of Arthur Jarvis on
October eighth, between eleven and twelve. Were you there
at that time?

ATTHEW   No, sir.

BURTON   Where were you?

MATTHEW   At Mrs. Ndela's, in End Street.

BURTON   You are sure of the time?

MATTHEW   Yes, sir. We had been dancing at the place in High Street, and
              when we came to Mrs. Ndela's she said, "You are late, but
              come in," and we saw that it was near eleven.

BURTON   Do you know Absalom Kumalo?

MATTHEW   Yes, sir. He is the son of my father's brother.

BURTON   Was he with you on this evening?

MATTHEW   No, sir.

BURTON   Do you know where he was?

MATTHEW   No, sir.

BURTON   The witness is excused for the moment.
              [MATTHEW *steps back to the bench and sits*. BURTON *crosses*
              the judge]
              Your Honor, I am about to call the third defendant, Absalom
              Kumalo. Before I do so I wish to explain that his plea o
              guilty is his own choice, and that I have not attempted t
              influence him in any way.

JUDGE   I understand, sir. You may proceed.

BURTON   Absalom Kumalo, will take the stand.
              [ABSALOM *does so*]
              Absalom Kumalo, you are accused of being one of thre
              masked men who entered the kitchen of Arthur Jarvis o
              October eighth, between eleven and twelve in the evenin
              Were you there at that time?

ABSALOM   Yes, sir.

RTON   Who were the two masked men with you?

SALOM   Matthew Kumalo and Johannes Pafuri.

RTON   What was your purpose in going there?

SALOM   To steal something from the house.

RTON   Why did you choose this day?

SALOM   Because Johannes said the house would be empty at that time.

RTON   This same Johannes Pafuri here?

SALOM   Yes, sir.

RTON   When did you three go to this house?

SALOM   It was after eleven at night.

RTON   Did you go there disguised?

SALOM   We tied handkerchiefs over our mouths.

RTON   And then?

SALOM   We went into the kitchen and there was a servant there.

RTON   This man?

SALOM   Yes, that is the man.

RTON   Tell the court what happened then.

SALOM   This man was afraid. He saw my revolver. He said, "What do
          you want?" Johannes said, "We want money and clothes."
          This man said, "You cannot do such a thing." Johannes said,
          "Do you want to die?" Then this man called out, "Master!
          Master!" and Johannes struck him over the head with the
          iron bar.

BURTON   Did he call again?

ABSALOM   He made no sound.

BURTON   What did you do?

ABSALOM   No, we were silent—and listened.

BURTON   Where was your revolver?

ABSALOM   In my hand.

BURTON   And then?

ABSALOM   Then a white man came into the doorway.

BURTON   And then?

ABSALOM   I was frightened. I fired the revolver.

BURTON   And then?

ABSALOM   The white man fell.

BURTON   And then?

ABSALOM   Matthew said, "We must go." So we all went quickly.

BURTON   Where did you go?

ABSALOM   I wandered about. I wanted to find a place to hide.

JUDGE   I have a question to ask, Mr. Burton.

BURTON   Yes, Your Honor.

JUDGE   Why did you carry a revolver?

ABSALOM   It was to frighten the servant of the house.

JUDGE   Where did you get this revolver?

ABSALOM   I bought it from a man.

JUDGE   Was this revolver loaded when you bought it?

ABSALOM   It had two bullets in it.

JUDGE   How many bullets were in it when you went to this house?

ABSALOM   One.

JUDGE   What happened to the other?

ABSALOM   I took the revolver out into the hills and fired it.

JUDGE   What did you fire at?

ABSALOM   I fired at a tree.

JUDGE   Did you hit this tree?

ABSALOM   Yes, I hit it.

JUDGE   Then you thought, "Now I can fire this revolver"?

ABSALOM   Yes, that is so.

JUDGE   And when Matthew Kumalo and Johannes Pafuri say they were not with you at the time of the murder they are lying?

ABSALOM   Yes, they are lying.

JUDGE   Do you know where they went after the crime?

ABSALOM   No, I do not know.

JUDGE   Where did you go?

ABSALOM   I went to a plantation and buried the revolver.

JUDGE   And what did you do next?

ABSALOM   I prayed there.

JUDGE   What did you pray there?

ABSALOM   I prayed for forgiveness.

JUDGE   How did the police find you?

ABSALOM   Johannes Pafuri brought them to where I was.

JUDGE   And what did you tell them?

ABSALOM   I told them it was not Johannes who had killed the whit
            man, it was I myself.

JUDGE   And how was the revolver found?

ABSALOM   No, I told the police where to find it.

JUDGE   And every word you have said is true?

ABSALOM   Every word is true.

JUDGE   There is no lie in it?

ABSALOM   There is no lie in it, for I said to myself, I shall not lie an
            more, all the rest of my days, nor do anything more that
            evil.

JUDGE   In fact, you repented.

ABSALOM   Yes, I repented.

JUDGE   Because you were in trouble?

ABSALOM   Yes, because I was in trouble.

JUDGE   Did you have any other reason for repenting?

ABSALOM   No, I had no other reason.

JUDGE   I have no further questions, Mr. Burton.

BURTON   The witness is dismissed.

            [*The lights dim on the courtroom, and the* CHORUS *comes forward*

CHORUS   [*Sings*]
And here again, in this place,
A man who has killed takes breath
With the fear of death in his face,
Fear of death for death,
And are the terms of justice clearly met?
Not yet, no, not quite yet.

[*The courtroom lights come up again. The spectators are stand-*
ing; the JUDGE *sits; they all sit except the three boys who are*
awaiting sentence]

JUDGE   The evidence in this case is in many ways inconclusive, un-
satisfactory, and fragmentary. Some of the witnesses are or
could be interested parties. Some of the accused appear to
have testified in collusion with each other or other witnesses.
There are many points not clear, some of which, perhaps, will
now never be clear. It seems quite possible that Matthew
Kumalo and Johannes Pafuri are guilty with Absalom
Kumalo of the murder of Arthur Jarvis. It was the identification of Pafuri by the servant who was struck that led to
Pafuri's arrest. It was the arrest of Pafuri that led the police
to arrest Absalom and later Matthew. The alibis offered by
Matthew and Johannes are obviously doubtful. No reason
has come to light why Absalom should involve in the robbery
and murder two men who were not with him at the time and
not guilty. And yet, after long and thoughtful consideration,
my assessors and I have come to the conclusion that the guilt
of Matthew and Johannes is not sufficiently established.
[MATTHEW *and* JOHANNES *look at each other, puzzled*]
There remains the case against Absalom Kumalo. Except for
his plea and his confession the case against him remains sub-
stantially that against Johannes and Matthew. His guilt is
not established in the testimony alone, but that testimony,
taken together with his confession, leads us inescapably to the
conclusion that he is guilty. No reason has been offered why
he should confess to a deed he did not commit, and his own
insistence that he had no intention to kill operates to validate
the confession itself. Matthew Kumalo and Johannes Pafuri,
you are discharged and may step down.
[*They do so, move over right quietly;* LINDA *and* ROSE *rise and*
join them]

Absalom Kumalo, have you anything to say before I pro
nounce sentence?

ABSALOM   I have only this to say, that I killed this man, but I did no
mean to kill him, only I was afraid.

JUDGE   Absalom Kumalo,
             [*The spectators lean toward the* JUDGE, *who puts a little black ca*
             on his head]
             I sentence you to be returned to custody, and to be hanged by
             the neck until you are dead. And may the Lord have mercy o
             your soul.

             [IRINA *rises, then* STEPHEN. JARVIS *gets up and crosses the court*
             room. As he does so he is met by STEPHEN. JARVIS *steps back to*
             let STEPHEN *pass. He goes to Absalom, who stands stunned and*
             motionless]

Act Two

The prison cell. The lights come up on the chorus.

CHORUS   [*Sings "Cry, the Beloved Country"*]
Cry, the beloved country,
Cry, the beloved land,
the wasted childhood,
the wasted youth,
the wasted man!
Cry, the broken tribes, and the broken hills,
and the right and wrong forsaken,
the greed that destroys us,
the birds that cry no more!
Cry, the beloved country,
Cry, the lost tribe, the lost son.

[*The* CHORUS *parts, revealing the prison cell. Absalom is in the cell, Irina near him.* STEPHEN *is reading the marriage service*]

STEPHEN   —to live together after God's ordinance in the holy estate of Matrimony? Wilt thou obey him, and serve him, love, honour, and keep him, and forsaking all others, keep thee only unto him, so long as ye both shall live?

IRINA   I will.

WOMAN   [*Sings*]
Cry, the unborn son,
the inheritor of our fear,
let him not laugh too gladly in the water of the clove,
nor stand too silent
when the setting sun makes the veld red with fire.

STEPHEN   And now you are man and wife, my son, and my daughter. Irina will come with me to Ndotsheni, Absalom.

ABSALOM   I am glad, my father.

STEPHEN   We shall care for your child as if it were our own.

ABSALOM   I thank you, my father.

STEPHEN   Will you wish to say good-by to Irina?

ABSALOM   There is no way to say good-by. My father, I must go to Pretoria.

STEPHEN   There will be an appeal.

ABSALOM   But it will not help. I am afraid. I am afraid of the hanging

STEPHEN   Be of courage, my son.

ABSALOM   It's no help to be of courage! O *Tixo*, *Tixo*, I am afraid of th rope and the hanging!

[IRINA *kneels*]

GUARD   You must go now.

ABSALOM   Where I go there will be no wife or child or father or mothe There is no food taken or given! And no marriage! Where I go O *Tixo*, *Tixo*!

CHORUS   [*Sings*]
            Cry, the unborn son,
            fatherless,
            let him not be moved by the song of the bird,
            nor give his heart to a mountain
            nor to a valley!

            Cry, the beloved country!
            Cry, the lost son,
            the lost tribe—
            the lost—
            The great red hills stand desolate,
            and the earth has torn away like flesh.
            These are the valleys
            Of old men and old women,
            of mothers and children.

WOMAN   [*Sings*]
            Cry, the beloved land.

[*The lights dim*]

Act Two

the lights come up we see Alex playing with a little Negro boy and girl.
ere is a small handmade toy between them. We can see the interior of the
pel, center stage.

EX   [*Sings "Big Mole"*]
Big Mole was a digger of the fastest kind;
He'd dig in the earth like you think in your mind;
When Big Mole came to the side of a hill
Instead of going over he'd start in to drill.
He promised his mother a well in the town
And he brought boiling water from a thousand feet down!

Down, down, down, down,
Three mile, four mile, five mile down;
He can go through rock, he can go through coal;
Whenever you come to an oversize hole
Down at the bottom is Big Black Mole!
Big Black Mole, Big Black Mole!

When Mole was a younker they showed him a mine;
He said, "I like the idea fine,
Let me have that hose, let me have that drill."
If they hadn't shut it off he'd be boring still!
And down at the bottom he chunked all around
Till he chunked out a city six mile in the ground!

Down, down, down, down,
Three mile, four mile, five mile down;
You can bet your pants, you can bet your soul,
Whenever you come to a main-size hole
Down at the bottom is Big Black Mole!
Big Black Mole! Big Black Mole!

Big Mole had a girl who was small and sweet;
He promised her diamonds for her hands and feet;
He dug so deep and he dug so well,
He broke right into the ceiling of hell,

75

And he looked the old devil spang in the eye,
And he said, "I'm not coming back here till I die!"

[EDWARD JARVIS *enters and stands listening*]

ALEX   [*Sings*]
              Down, down, down, down,
              Three mile, four mile, five mile down;
              He can go through rock, he can go through coal;
              Whenever you come to a sure-enough hole,
              Down at the bottom is Big Black Mole!
              Big Black Mole, Big Black Mole, Big Black Mole!

EDWARD   Hi, there!

ALEX   Hi.

[*The other two* CHILDREN *get up and run off to the right*]

EDWARD   You know, there's one thing I have to say for your voice
              it's loud. It reminds me of Jericho.

ALEX   Jericho?

EDWARD   Yes, the man that knocked the town over with music.

ALEX   It was Joshua that broke the walls of the city with musi
              Jericho was the name of the city he destroyed.

EDWARD   How do you know that?

ALEX   My uncle read it to me out of the Old Testament.

EDWARD   Well, don't sing as loud as you can around here, or some
              these walls might go down.

[EDWARD *laughs*, ALEX *joins him, they both laugh*]

ALEX   I'll be very careful, sir.

EDWARD   I'm waiting for my grandfather now. We live up there in tl
              hills.

EX   I know. I've seen you riding around up there. On a bicycle.

WARD   Sometimes I ride a bicycle, sometimes a horse. I can fall off both just fine.
[*They laugh again*]
What have you got there?

EX   A digging machine.

WARD   Does it work?

EX   Not much. I made it myself.

WARD   What's your name?

EX   Alex.

WARD   Mine's Edward. I guess your uncle's the umfundisi here.

EX   Yes, he is.

WARD   I know a lot of Zulu words. My father taught them to me. *Ingeli* is English.

LEX   That's right.

WARD   What's the word for water?

LEX   *Amanzi.*

DWARD   And how do you say to die?

LEX   *Siyafa.*

DWARD   The young *Ingeli siyafa* for *amanzi*—is that right?

LEX   You mean the English boy is dying for water?

DWARD   Uh-huh. I am, too. Only I'd rather have milk, out of the fridge.

LEX   The fridge?

EDWARD   You know, the refrigerator.

ALEX   My uncle doesn't have one.

EDWARD   How do you keep the milk cold?

ALEX   We have no milk. Nobody has milk in Ndotsheni.

EDWARD   No milk!

ALEX   No. Can I get you some water?

EDWARD   Never mind. [*To himself*] No milk. . . . You know, you'
          got a real idea here; if you had something heavy on th
          string, and it had a point on it, and it kept dropping on t
          ground, it would really dig.

ALEX   Like a nail?

          [JAMES JARVIS *enters from the left*]

JARVIS   We're going now, Edward.

EDWARD   Yes, Grandfather.

          [*He rises.* ALEX *rises*]

JARVIS   The car's at the market.

ALEX   [*Afraid of Jarvis*] I have to go.

          [*He runs to the right*]

EDWARD   Good-by, Alex!

ALEX   [*Stopping*] Good-by—Edward!

          [*He runs off behind the chapel, waves to* EDWARD, *who al
          waves farewell*]

JARVIS   Edward, when you are a man, you will live your own life. Yo
          will live as you please to live. But while you live with m
          never let me see this again.

EDWARD   You mean talking with this boy?

JARVIS   I mean that.

EDWARD   But I like him. He's bright and he's nice.

JARVIS   There are not many rules in my house. I am lax in many ways,
          and not easily angered.
          [*He sits—his head in his hands.* EDWARD *sits beside him*]
          I have lost so much that I don't know why I go on living, or
          what's worth saving. I don't know any more why any man
          should do his tasks or work for gain or love his child. I don't
          know why any child should obey—or whether good will come
          of it or evil. But I do know this; there are some things that I
          cannot bear to look on.

          [*We hear organ music. The lights come up in the chapel.*
          PARISHIONERS *come in from the right and take their places in the
          chapel.* STEPHEN *and* GRACE *enter. Stephen stands before the
          pulpit. Jarvis still sits on the step*]

STEPHEN   [*Speaking from the pulpit*] I will say first the hardest thing I
          have to say. I am resigning from my pastorate at Ndotsheni.
          I shall be your umfundisi no more. It had been my hope to
          end my years here, but—I cannot now.

EDWARD   Aren't we going, Grandfather?

JARVIS   We'll wait a moment.

STEPHEN   My son Absalom will die tomorrow morning on the scaffold
          for a murder to which he confessed, and of which he was
          guilty. You all know of this. The man he killed was known to
          you, too. He was Arthur Jarvis. He was born in the hills above
          our little town. There was a brightness upon him even as a
          child. As a man he was a friend of our race, a friend of all men,
          a man all men could be proud of. And my son—killed him.
          And the mother of Arthur Jarvis is dead of grief for her son.
          My people, if I stay here now I become a hindrance to you,
          and not a help. I must go.

PARISH-   You cannot go, umfundisi!
IONERS   You cannot go!
             No, umfundisi!

STEPHEN   This is a poor village, Ndotsheni, and it grows poorer. In th
             past when our little church was in desperate need we hav
             sometimes turned to Arthur Jarvis, and he has helped us. F
             will not help here again. And no one will help you while
             remain here, for the man who slew him was my son. I mu
             go for still another reason, my dear people. When I began
             serve my God and my church I had a sure faith that the Go
             of our world ordered things well for men. I had a sure fait
             that though there was good and evil I knew which was good
             and God knew it—and that men were better in their hear
             for choosing good and not evil. Something has shaken this i
             me. I am not sure of my faith. I am lost. I am not sure now.
             am not sure that we are not all lost. And a leader should no
             be lost. He should know the way, and so I resign my place

MCRAE   Umfundisi, if you have lost your faith, I too have lost m
             faith.

PARISH.   Yes.

MCRAE   Where does a man go, and what does he do when his faith i
             gone?

STEPHEN   I don't know.

PARISH.   Oh, Stephen, you have always helped us. Please stay!

STEPHEN   If I keep my place, and this black thing has happened to my
             son and is said, little by little the few who still worship here
             will shrink away, the rusty roof will leak more, the floor wil
             break till there is none, the windows will go—they will be
             thrown at and broken and will go—and the unpainted sides
             of this chapel I have loved will stand empty, roofless—and I
             shall live in despair beside it, knowing that I have done this
             thing to you and to my church by remaining.

             [STEPHEN starts to go—they all reach out to him and he pauses]

LLAGER [*Sings "A Bird of Passage"*]
        Lord of the heart, look down upon
            Our earthly pilgrimage,
        Look down upon us where we walk
            From bright dawn to old age,
        Give light not shed by any sun.

RISH.   Lord of the heart!

AN   Not read on any page.

HORUS   Lord of the heart!

        A bird of passage out of night
            Flies in at a lighted door,
        Flies through and on in its darkened flight
            And then is seen no more.
        [STEPHEN *stands for a moment at the pulpit, then turns and goes
        out*]
        This is the life of men on earth:
        Out of darkness we come at birth
        Into a lamplit room, and then—

DWARD   [*Speaking through the music*] What is it, Grandfather?

HORUS   [*Sings*]
        Go forward into dark again,
        Go forward into dark again.

        [*The lights dim*]

Act Two

It is before daylight the next morning and Stephen is sitting on a chair i
front of the table in the room where we saw him in the first scene of the pla
There is an extra chair upstage center added to this scene. Stephen sits watc
ing the clock on the shelf. The CHORUS sings as the lights come up.

CHORUS   Four o'clock, it will soon be four.

IRINA   [*Coming in*] Umfundisi.

STEPHEN   Yes, Irina?

IRINA   She has fallen asleep. She meant to sit and watch with yc
at this hour, and she has been awake till only now—but no
she sleeps.

STEPHEN   We won't wake her, Irina. If she sleeps and the hour go
past, then at least it will be past.

IRINA   Even in her sleep she reaches for my hand.

STEPHEN   Sit beside her, Irina, if you can.

IRINA   Yes, I can.

[*She starts to go.* STEPHEN *stops her*]

STEPHEN   My daughter, I'm glad he found you and not some other.

IRINA   I'm glad he found me, my father.

[*She goes back into the kitchen*]

CHORUS   [*Sings*]
Four o'clock, it will soon be four.

LEADER   [*Sings*]
Why do they choose the morning,
the morning, when men sleep sound?

HORUS   [*Sings*]
            Four o'clock,
            it will soon be four.

STEPHEN   [*Speaks*]
            If they would kill me instead
            Absalom would make a good man.
            But it will never be.
            He is waiting now.
            Sleep, O mother. Sleep sound.
            Soon Absalom will sleep.
            [JARVIS *enters from left, crosses to door, knocks.* STEPHEN, *almost
            unaware of what he is doing, answers*]
            Yes—

JARVIS   [*In the doorway*] I hope you will forgive me for coming at this
            hour, umfundisi.

STEPHEN   [*Rising*] Why are you here?

JARVIS   May I come in?

STEPHEN   You—you wish to come into my house?

JARVIS   Yes.

STEPHEN   Come in, sir.

JARVIS   [*Entering*] I stood outside your church yesterday and heard
            what you said to your people, and what they said to you. I
            want you to know that I will help you with the roof and with
            the painting—and whatever must be done. I will do whatever
            my son would have done.

STEPHEN   I—thank you, sir. The church will thank you.

JARVIS   Whatever you need.

STEPHEN   Mr. Jarvis.
            [*He looks at the clock*]
            It's hard for me to think of the church or of—in a quarter of
            an hour my son is to die.

JARVIS   I know. I couldn't sleep—thinking of it.

STEPHEN   I think this does not touch you.

JARVIS   Yes. It does.

STEPHEN   I don't know how. I think it might be better if I sat her
             alone.

JARVIS   I know my presence pains you. I know I am the last ma
             in the world you wish to see. And yet—may I stay for
             moment?

STEPHEN   If you wish.

JARVIS   Stephen Kumalo, my wife is dead. My son is dead. I live in
             house with a child who knows me only as an old man. I hav
             thought many times I would be better dead. I thought my
             self alone in this desolation that used to be my home. Bu
             when I heard you yesterday I knew that your grief an
             mine were the same. I know now that of all the men who liv
             near this great valley you are the one I would want for
             friend. And—I have been walking about—and came an
             knocked here now—because I wanted to sit with you i
             this hour—

STEPHEN   You want to sit with me?

JARVIS   Yes, if I may.

STEPHEN   Mr. Jarvis, you know that you can give me only charit
             If you were seen to touch my hand, this town, this who
             valley, would turn against you.

JARVIS   I've finished with that. I haven't come here lightly. I sha
             take your hand wherever I like, before whom I like. I sha
             come and worship in your church if I wish to worship. May
             sit here with you?

STEPHEN   Yes, umnumzana.
             [JARVIS *starts to sit*]
             This is not a good chair.
             [*He brings another chair and places it.* JARVIS *sits*]
             It's almost the hour. O God—O *Tixo*—it is almost now.

ARVIS   But there will be a tomorrow, Stephen. Edward will come
           tomorrow to see Alex. He wants to come and play.

TEPHEN   I shall be gone. I shall never see this place again. Nor the
           path where Absalom ran to meet me—nor the hills where he
           played and came late to supper—nor the room where he
           slept—never, never again.

ARVIS   You must stay in Ndotsheni.

TEPHEN   If I stayed, do you know what I would preach here? That
           good can come from evil, and evil from good! That no man
           knows surely what is evil or what is good! That if there is a
           God He is hidden and has not spoken to men! That we are
           all lost here, black and white, rich and poor, the fools and
           the wise! Lost and hopeless and condemned on this rock that
           goes 'round the sun without meaning!

ARVIS   Not hopeless, Stephen, and not without meaning. For even
           out of the horror of this crime some things have come that
           are gain and not loss. My son's words to me and my under-
           standing of my son. And your words in the chapel, and my
           understanding of those words—and your son's face in the
           courtroom when he said he would not lie any more or do any
           evil. I shall never forget that.

TEPHEN   You think well of my son?

ARVIS   I tried not to. But you and I have never had to face what
           Absalom faced there. A man can hardly do better than he did
           when he stood before the judge. Stay in Ndotsheni, Stephen,
           stay with those who cried out to you in the chapel. You have
           something to give them that nobody else can give them. And
           you can be proud of Absalom.

TEPHEN   And he is forgiven, and I am forgiven?

ARVIS   Let us forgive each other.

TEPHEN   Umnumzana—umnumzana!

ARVIS   Let us be neighbors. Let us be friends.

STEPHEN   Umnumzana—before the clock strikes—I shall stay i
Ndotsheni. You are welcome in this house. I have a friend.

JARVIS   I have a friend.

[*The clock strikes four.* STEPHEN *sits and buries his head in h
hands.* JARVIS *goes to him, puts an arm around him*]

CHORUS   [*Sings*]
Each lives alone in a world of dark,
Crossing the skies in a lonely arc,
Save when love leaps out like a leaping spark
Over thousands, thousands of miles!

CURTAIN